THE END OF SUFFERING
AND THE PATH TO SUPREME ILLUMINATION

BY LEWIS ABDULLAH CATTELL

Published by Lewis Abdullah Cattell Self-Publishing
Website: www.lewisabdullahcattell.com
Email: info@lewisabdullahcattell.com

ISBN: 9798622503634

Cover design and typography by Lewis Cattell
Cover photo by Hristo Fidanov from Pexels

Dedicated to every seeker

Contents

AUTHORS INTRODUCTION

This book is a spiritual treatise in the form of prose and parable. It is about the path toward attaining gnosis – inner communion with God, the Divine Essence.

It is a story of cycles, within higher cycles; reaching to increasingly profound states, until the idol of the individuated 'I' is removed, and the light of The Divine can fully illuminate the inner-self.

In part, it is a dialogue on spirituality, and in part, a discussion about human ethics, which extend beyond the realms of mere legalities, and considers enlightened ideals of human behaviour – the pinnacle of which is to create abundant good and no harm. It is intended to give an alternative perspective on the context in which scriptures are interpreted - suggesting that the purpose of scripture is not to form organised religion as it exists today, or to create authority systems and hierarchy, or even to propagate dogmatism or tribalism/sectarianism. Instead, its purpose is to call us back to a state of inner-communion with our source – God, The Divine Essence, or whatever name you choose to call It.

The discussions in this story, are intended to challenge accepted norms, and break down preconceptions. This is because, in the experience of unity, all preconceptions are obliterated before the face of The Divine. Meaning that everything you think you know is only a partial manifestation of the ultimate truth, which is transcendent in nature and remains perpetually out of the reach of thought and mental understanding.

I have purposefully kept the main character, The Wayfarer, genderless and I have done the same with any references to God or the Divine Essence - any references to their gender that you may find in the text are unintentional. I hope that this empowers both genders to identify fully with the main character and to become empowered in their relationship with The Divine.

If this book challenges your perceptions, preconceptions or fixed ideas in any way, please embrace it, meditate on it, and savour that process. I hope you will enjoy the story and benefit immensely from it. But most of all, I hope you will turn yourself fully to the source of all existence, surrendering to its endless and profound outpouring of love and guidance.

Lewis Abdullah Cattell

THE END OF SUFFERING

AND THE PATH TO SUPREME ILLUMINATION

"Tear aside the veils of all you see in this world, and you will find yourself alone in solitude with God. If you draw aside the veils of the stars and the spheres, you will see that all is one with the Essence of your own pure soul. If you will but tear aside the veil, you will see nonexistence, and you will see forthwith the true meaning of God's purpose. When you have cast aside the veil, you will see the Essence, and all things will be shown forth within the Essence. If you draw aside the veil from the Face of the Beloved, all that is hidden will be made manifest, and you will become one with God..."

— Farid al-Din Attar, Persian Poet, 1145 – c. 1221

CHAPTER 1

THE WAYFARER

1. Be still, and witness the sublime name of God; unspeakable, unspoken. The one who proclaims it diverts far from it; the one who knows it - is silenced by awe. Minds are not capable of encompassing it. Lips are not capable of uttering it. The heart is enraptured before it. Prostrate then, your entire being before the majesty of its Holy Mystery.

2. On a boat between two oceans, gliding through the rhythmic waves as if it were a magnificent fish, a Wayfarer stood like an outpouring beaker of love, fondly observing the emerging vision of the shore. Leaning on a flowering cane, and wrapped in an unhemmed sheet, brilliantly white

and undulating in the gentle breeze, the Wayfarer stood motionless - as if exhaled from the Divine Presence Itself.

3. To the onlookers on the shore, it appeared as if a shining star had risen upon the horizon. The people were enthralled in awe. Whether standing, sitting or lying, they became like statues from a bygone age.

4. In the complete and deafening silence, the vessel reached its place of rest on the shores of this secluded island - alone in the vast emptiness, sat between two endless oceans.

5. The people thronged with excitement as the boat serenely reached its mooring. As the Wayfarer silently stepped forth, a feeling of eerie otherworldliness hung in the air.

A young and somewhat scraggly seven-year-old child grasped the Wayfarer's warm hand, as a pungent smell of delicate perfume, and heavenly incense rippled through the warm morning air.

The people stared, open-mouthed as if they were looking through a doorway into another reality.

From amongst the crowd, the fishermen protectively stepped forward, ushering the people back as if they feared a greater danger than this stranger could ever possibly enact. They were brawny, muscular men, whose faces had become deeply weathered by years at sea.

A heavy-set man from amongst them, called Tasawwur (imagination) spoke up in a harsh, raspy voice, "Stranger, from which kingdom have you come? These oceans are vast, and you are unmarked by your journey; this is a strange sight - explain yourself!"

6. The Wayfarer crouched down and embraced the young child, and then looking up at the crowd, replied to Tasawwur, "Like a child of seven years, I have come from a kingdom without shores. Ask not where I am from, less you would place between us, within yourself, a division. 7. Rather, know that I have overcome the two oceans and now I am amongst you – so that you too may overcome."

8. The people looked at each other, dismayed by these strange words. Tassawur replied, "Our catch is meagre, and our ships are unsound, due to years of being relentlessly beaten by the waves; the King burdens us with heavy taxes, and the priests demand their share; the scholars condemn us, while the lawmakers place endless restrictions upon us - the stomachs of the people hunger, and their bodies are sullied and weak… How then can we overcome anything?

9. The Wayfarer said, "You who have recognised these wrongs shall right them. For if you first cast the net within, your catch will be more fruitful than the greatest harvest. Therefore, do not fear your ineptitude, as the Sustainer of All is the disposer of your every thought. But know this: The waves you create, shall pound relentlessly upon the vessels of many others. So as you have complained of others, so too even the fish in the depths of the oceans complain of you. Do not cause harm, and rectify harm wherever you find it. Because for the one who saves a life, it is as if they have saved all lives. Therefore I urge you: Do not await a saviour, rather be one to all who are in need."

10. The Wayfarer began to walk along the wooden harbour to the shore, with the growing crowd thronging around. An archer from amongst those gathered climbed up upon the base of a stone pylon and shouted out, "Wayfarer, forgive our inhospitality, come into our city and feast with us! We have many lodgings and can provide you with food. Where would you prefer to be received?"

11. The Wayfarer replied, "Blessed is the one who listens and comprehends; a guide for the seeker, a shelter for the helpless. I shall feast with you who have invited me, and share in the joy of the one who gives; for the only way

a cup can give to the one who fills it, is to be filled for the joy of being emptied by their lips."

12. As the Wayfarer moved onward, the crowd vibrated with a low hum of words. Then the Wayfarer spoke again, saying, "I shall stay with you, to the contentment of your hearts, but you must know, my destination before the day is through, is the Temple of Man."

CHAPTER 2

THE HARLOT

13. As they reached the city streets, the foul smell of sewage and scattered refuse hung heavily in the air. Then from amongst the crowd, a harlot, Mukhliṣa (Sincerity) pushed her way forward. The people of the city despaired at her, and tried to hold her back, saying, "The impure should not come near the pure!"

14. However, the Wayfarer said, "Let her be!" Then walked to her, held her hands, and said, "Who is more impure than the one who takes another's dignity from them? Are those who have not bathed in the waters of empathy truly clean?"

15. Trembling and squinting with one eye, as if she feared the sting of a striking hand, Mukhliṣa said, "I think you are deftly wise – you're the one told of by the priestly folk of old!"

She squeezed the Wayfarer's hands as if an intangible pain was overcoming her. Then she pointed at the crowd around saying, "These never let me forget that I'm the lowest of this city! Wayfarer, I fear you will judge me harsh! But know this…"

16. She paused to inhale a breath that was thick with heavy emotion. Then, as if she had found a new force of life, she said, "I am the secret of the nobles, politicians, and priestly folk - abused by all men and protected by no women. 17. Each night I repent one thousand times, and each morning I am abused again! Tell me my fate, for what can be worse than what I have already endured?"

18. The Wayfarer embraced Mukhliṣa full of compassion, kissed her hands and said, "No longer shall you be abused, for I shall raise you higher than the nobles; into the purifying waters of Divine Intimacy. 19. Yet know, just as the nobles from the heights of the city have abused you, so too have the thoughts of your imagination; by arousing the desires of the flesh. But now, *that* desire shall bathe in the mystery of God's unspeakable name, and your mind shall ascend to It; as if a virginal spirit."

20. The Wayfarer then took off Mukhliṣa's worn, black cloak and placed a mantle of undyed hemp upon her shoulders.

Mukhliṣa gasped and said, "I see within me light, where before I could not see!"

21. She then took her black cloak and placed it over the shoulders of the Wayfarer and with an air of wonder she said, "Whatever mystery you are, I shall serve you!"

22. Pulling the cloak on, the Wayfarer said, "As you think, so shall it be. So think good and you shall accomplish your task."

Then, turning to the people, the Wayfarer said, "The streets of your neighbourhood are soiled with the excrement from your bodies. Yet you curse the streets, whist you have clean hands, but sullied minds. Instead of cursing the streets clean your thoughts, and labour with dirtied hands until no filth nor odour remains.

23. "I tell you, when enmity and disdain enter the heart, it is even harder to remove the odour; even once the heart is cleansed! Therefore, do not revile the unfortunate amongst you, but rather raise them, and lower yourselves. 24. Give them refuge when no refuge can be found. Indeed,

there is no refuge; except within the blissful communion of the silent heart."

CHAPTER 3

THE CHAMBER

25. The people became fearful and said, "Beware, This is the one who the priest and scholars have warned us about: The heavenly judge who shall weight our hearts, and cast the wrongdoers into a burning fire!"

26. Tears welled in the eyes of the Wayfarer who replied, "Do not fear me; rather fear yourselves - for your hearts are the thrones of God. Yet you have evicted The Supreme Divinity and enthroned the desires and emotions of your flesh. So now I say to you, abdicate the throne so that the Unspeakable Light may be established firmly upon it! Then balance shall be returned, and fear itself shall be banished from the kingdom altogether."

27. The people wept for shame, wailing, "We have ruined the innocence of our hearts - we confess! Surely you are the one that was prophesied, in days gone by!"

28. The sound of wailing reached up to the highest walls and towers of the keep. Suddenly the assembly of the court were roused. The Priests, Judges and Scholars rushed down the city steps toward the weeping crowd, as if a fearsome army was charging into battle.

29. As the mob grew and the people surged, the young maiden Rahm (Womb) beckoned the Wayfarer, "Come quickly now into my chamber, and I shall give you refuge until the crowd has settled down."

30. When the door had closed, the maiden questioned the Wayfarer, "Tell me, please, are you the one that they speak of, from the ancient prophecies?"

The Wayfarer sat cross-legged, with closed eyes, in the centre of the dimly lit room and said, "The hearts of Mankind are like cups, which pour forth that which they contain within them. If these cups are emptied and thoroughly cleansed, they will become containers of sweetness, yet if they become filled with bitterness - no amount of sweetness can disguise the foul taste. 31. All who speak, pour forth the contents of their heart; then all that is hidden, shall be revealed - to the one who comprehends. Therefore I say to you, do not wonder about the words of men; rather empty your cup and clean it thoroughly, so that you may taste the sweetness poured forth from The Divine Presence.

32. "I tell you, a name is a doorway to the reality of a thing - so you may call me by many names. For my reality is one, yet it may be approached, through many doors. Therefore if you call me Good Thought or Loving Compassion; then the doors, which you open, are vast. 33. As for the Supreme Divinity, Its name may not be spoken by lips or hearts for the door of its reality has no boundary and is never closed."

34. Rahm shyly spoke saying, "You are a great soul, full of wisdom; so tell me of marriage and a woman's place in the world?"

The Wayfarer replied, "One who owns a flawless diamond does not hold it aloft within a den of thieves. For it will be taken from them. They disclose such wealth only to one who has proven their trust and vowed to safeguard it; so it should be with your innocence and your loving heart.

35. "Indeed, both male and female were created from one soul, and one soul they shall become again. Therefore in the unity of the male and the female is the union of all

opposites, and from this unity comes forth the birth of the pure child.

"So I say to you, enter the wedding chamber, within and without. For, what is inside of you is also outside of you, and what is outside of you is also within.

36. "Your place in this world is the world. For just as you are in it, it is similarly within you.

"Indeed, the woman is the counterpart of the man, opposites in varying degrees, and an equalising force through which balance is attained, in every domain. Therefore do not seek to be like men, and do not allow yourself to be subjugated by them. Let your womanhood flourish to the fruition of its perfection, and shun any who would try to extinguish your light."

CHAPTER 4

THE REFUGE

37. At this moment Rahm's mother Walada (Birth) knocked at the door; wrapped in a cloak that shimmered like a peacocks tail. She said, "The people await you and will not leave! They prepare a feast for you in the city square. But take great care, for surely their longing for your wise words will greatly anger the King! This chamber of my daughter is no place for you, and though I fear there is no refuge for you in this city, I must insist that you leave her home!"

38. The Wayfarer turned to Walada and said, "O you, helplessly adrift upon the pounding waves of cause and effect. Come, take refuge in the stillness of your surrendering heart and the eternal spaciousness of your mind at rest.

39. "Release every thought, allowing yourself to drift upon the breezes of your awareness. Do not try to restrict

that which is infinitely vast, nor madly cling to that which flows like water from the Divine Source.

40. "In stillness await the dawning of inner light; rising like a chorus from the silence of the heart and mind. 41. For as daybreak brings refuge from the darkness of the night; so too the Divine Light dispels ignorance and fear. Therefore disperse the relentless chatter of neurotic thoughts; for the light of dawn has come."

42. Walada responded, "I only fear because I know that the dangers of the world are real; my fears protect me against harm! It is foolery to ignore such promptings!"

The Wayfarer replied, "Surely the mind's chatter presents itself as a great aid to your existence, but it is, in fact, great whispering darkness, which clouds the mind and distracts the heart from inner sight. Fear is the child of ignorance, and neither fear nor ignorance can enter the stillness of pristine communion. O Walada, be still and take sanctuary within the light!"

43. With a look of awe upon her face, Walada said, "Now I know you with greater certainty than I know my own child. If you are postponed any longer because of me - I will be ruined! Take my peacock cloak, and leave for the city square."

44. Exchanging mantles, the Wayfarer said, "I shall take your cloak so I may step forth unhindered, and it shall serve me like a chariot that will take me at a great speed.

45. "Now take ablution in the waters of inner communion and sow good thoughts like flowering seeds as you sit before the King of Kings." 46. At this, the Wayfarer stood up to leave, leaning upon the flowering cane.

47. Walada said, "Outside are my two sons - twins. They await you and will show you the way to the city square."

48. The Wayfarer stepped out from the door of the house, unnoticed amongst the tumultuous noise. The twins led the way up the city steps, toward the great pillared square, where the people began to gather in crowds.

CHAPTER 5

THE BEGGAR BY THE POOL

49. As they began to ascend, they reached the pool which fed the city with water. This reservoir itself was fed by two lightly trickling streams, which arose in the heights of the island as two springs, within the courtyard of the temple of man.

The water trickling into the pool was pure; however, the water in the pool was murky and stagnant. Twelve outlets fed the city with water, yet many of its outlets had been purposefully blocked, others had become clogged with debris, dirt and grime.

Around the edge of the pool walked two guards; Ju (Hunger) and Dhama (Thirst), both of which were prohibiting a beggar from drinking the water.

50. As the Wayfarer reached the pool, the beggar raised a loud petition, "Stranger! Help me! Help! I'm thirsty and need to wash my self - I am in desperate need.

Please draw water for me from the cistern, as the guards have prohibited me from coming near to it."

51. The Wayfarer asked the beggar his name. He replied in a distressed voice almost whimpering, "Faqir (poverty-stricken), my name is Faqir!"

The two conversed as the guards approached them ominously. The Wayfarer asked the guards, "Why has Faqir been prohibited from drinking this water?"

Ju replied, "This pool is the property of the King. It will become disease-ridden if the beggars and lowly people drink from it, and use its water for bathing. We are protecting it from them, and have dammed their outlets so that they cannot pollute it anymore."

52. The Wayfarer said, "The dust of Faqir has not polluted your pool - rather *you* have polluted it with your minds. For when flowing water and a dirty body mix, the body is cleaned, and the water washes away the dirt it contains - becoming pure once again. However, when the flow of water is restricted, stagnation occurs. Similarly, all life must exist in a perpetual flow of cycles. For if it stops, death and decay rapidly takes hold. Therefore, through *your* ignorance and prejudice, it is *you* who have defiled the waters of life for all - so desist!"

53. Dumfounded Ju and Dhama replied, "Forgive us for our iniquity! We acted only as guardians so that to the best of our abilities these waters would not become ruined."

54. The Wayfarer said, "Do not fear loss, for those who are thankful shall be increased; and do not let greed possess you, for ravenous desire will intoxicate your mind while robbing empathy from your loving heart.

"Do not restrict the blessings, which flow from the Divine Source like a love song. For all of humankind are sovereigns, worthy of the greatest of treasures. All beings exist to receive sublime goodness; indeed, each of Mankind is a vice-regent of the Divine Sovereign. Therefore, it is your duty, to direct divine blessings, through good thought, without restriction.

55. "Indeed, within acts of kindness, compassion, and mutual co-operation, there is hidden greater wealth than in all of the resources that you could ever accumulate. Indeed, in charity is purification; as it eliminates stagnation within the heart whilst raising the helpless and needy to improved conditions.

"Outer charity is to selflessly fulfil the needs of those who are poverty-stricken and powerless, while inner charity elevates the mind to good thoughts; and the soul to the intimacy of divine gnosis. So, live by way of mutual co-operation, raising one another to increasingly perfected conditions and states."

56. Ju said, "What you have said is great indeed; I have never heard the like of it. Your words have washed away greed and contempt from my heart." Pausing thoughtfully he continued, "What would you have us do? Please help us, because soon the people will become sick due to the increasing foulness of this water."

57. The Wayfarer said, "Let Faqir, the beggar drink!" Ju and Dhama looked at each other uneasily. Overcoming their reluctance, they signalled to Faqir and said, "Drink! Drink!" in voices full of urgency.

Faqir drank from the pure water trickling into the pool. In between each gulp, he said, "Forgive me! Bless you! Forgive me!"

Once he had finished drinking, the Wayfarer said, "Now let Faqir the beggar bathe!"

Dhama weakly protested, saying, "He is dirty! Please, stranger, have mercy!" But Ju placed his hand on Dhama's arms, and said, "Dhama, my comrade, my dear friend! Trust this Wayfarer, for within me, this stranger has sparked a light which I can hardly bear. Trust me, my brother; let this beggar bathe!" Even though it was a struggle for him, Dhama relented and in a defeated voice said, "Go ahead, beggar... you may bathe!"

Faqir entered the pool with his clothing on, vigorously washing, swimming and splashing, overcome with joy. The turbulence of the water naturally broke the dams restricting the pipes, and the water burst forth, clearing the stagnation in an instant; as the water flowed freely to all in need.

58. Faqir emerged from the pool, completely purified, as if baptised, in both the body and the spirit. The water too was pristinely pure and crystal clear. He then dropped to his knees, holding the two hands of the Wayfarer while he wept.

The two twins and the two guards then drank from the pure water of the pool.

59. The Wayfarer said, "Keep your pool clean; each morning and evening remove its silt and debris, keeping its waters flowing without restriction. If you cannot clean it daily, then clean it for three days, each month. For as you look for your sign in the heavens, there you shall find the moon. I say to you, think good thoughts and rectify your deeply rooted opinions. Enact goodness with your limbs and do not co-operate with evil; for when you have taken

upon yourself the body of the cosmos, you shall look upon what you have evoked through negative thoughts and weep, asking for forgiveness. So wash in the waters of empathy and compassion, and enact kindness for the benefit of all life."

60. All five of those present spoke beautiful words of praise for the Wayfarer. The last to speak was Dhama who said, "You have opened in us a great truth, as well as loving empathy, and unbridled compassion; and indeed a light has manifested deeply within our hearts.

"We swear we will eat and drink only that which we need of the beautiful plants and clean water. We shall feed the needy amongst us; for this is what the light compels us to do.

"We shall keep this pool clean so that all shall have pure water. Never shall we restrict that which The Divine has let flow abundantly, and for this, we are truly grateful."

At this, the five ascended the remaining steps together, as they continued toward the city square.

CHAPTER 6

THE CIRCLE IN THE SQUARE

61. As they reached the Square, they entered through an enormous arched gate crowned with a powerfully carved lion. The Wayfarer walked through the crowds who were gathering and sat in the heart of the square. Seeing this, the people formed a great circle all around. 62. The wealthy came down from the heights of the city and the poor ascended from the streets below. Everyone sat together, eagerly awaiting the wisdom of this stranger in their midst.

63. The atmosphere was tense and full of excitement; like an intense flame was burning deep inside of every heart. The Wayfarer sat in silence until the smell of finely cooked food and aromatic herbs began to spread upon the breeze.

64. Removing the cloak like the spreading of a peacocks tail, the Wayfarer smiled and said, "Let us feast together; for the one who is thankful shall be increased, the one who serves does so for the betterment of their soul, and the one who receives does so for the joy of the giver."

The crowd buzzed with voices as the people began to speak. 65. The scholars stood up amongst the multitude; the suspicion in their minds was visible within their eyes. They felt threatened, like cornered animals, and as much as they tried to disguise it, it exuded from their every breath.

The head scholar Aqedah (Dogma/Creed) spoke in a booming voice saying, "We must lay before this stranger a series of tests, for we fear this is an imposter who seeks to bring the established order into disarray! Who is this person, and what is their lineage? We are the authority in matters of religion, so only through us will you know the truth!"

66. The Wayfarer waited patiently as the other scholars spoke in turn, each labouring with extensive monologues, to make the people doubt and reject the newcomer before them.

Then once they had worn out their tongues and fatigued their minds, the Wayfarer spoke saying, "In truth, there is no religion, except for peaceful surrender to the Unspeakable Essence, which pours forth love and tenderness without end.

"You claim authority, yet the silent heart holds power in the realm of the flesh, and it is the soul that holds power in the field of the spirit; which domain do you have control over, other than your own delusions? Have you forgotten that the Unspeakable Essence is the authority over all?

67. "As for who I am; if you do not know me when I am with you, I shall never be known to you. For you have looked at descriptions, prophecies, and lineages written by man's hands; yet you have failed to look at what has been written by the Divine Author within your hearts. So even though you cast your eyes up to the heavens in prayer, you fail to see the signs engraved therein.

68. "Sincerely, I tell you; close your eyes, so that you may truly see. For the knowledge which exists within books will be rendered useless, when gnosis arises within the heart and soul."

69. "This is Blasphemy!" Shouted Aqedah, "Your own words have betrayed you! You have rejected the books of God!"

70. Undisturbed by this outburst, the Wayfarer smiled and softly said, "It is not I that have rejected, but rather, the rejecter is he who neglects what is within him, as well as that which is before his face. So if I have spoken sacrilegiously, it is against the intellects of men, and it is so as not to blaspheme against the source of all existence. For when the light of gnosis arises in the heart, all meanings are made clear, and all confusion is extinguished.

"I ask you: Now that the truth has come, and falsehood has passed away forever, what will you do?"

71. Aqedah looked pale and began to weep. After some time he wiped the tears from his face and said, "I did not hear this from my teachers, though as you have spoken it, I have found something I cannot yet bear, dawning in my heart. Who are you who says these things?"

72. The Wayfarer stood like a dazzling white light and said, "I have come to share with you the draught of The Divine Presence, yet I have found you drunk upon the world of men! Surely, transformation is hard for stones of ore, until they surrender to the flame of the crucible. But surrender they must if they are to become silver and gold. As for me, I am like the pen of a great author; for what the

author wills, the pen shall inscribe within the pages of your hearts."

CHAPTER 7

THE REFINER

73. The feast began, and the people rejoiced: Eating and drinking and singing with joy. Then from amongst the people, a finely dressed and charismatic man moved toward the Wayfarer.

Once he was close enough, the man half-bowed, waving his arms around as if he was trying to emphasise his humility. Then bowing down on one knee, with his arms raised as if in prayer, he said, "O honoured one! O great and all-wise prophet! O you endowed of power and might; bestower of great authority and guidance! I Makara (Plot/Scheme) the great minister of this city honour you! Please! O you! Great teacher! Tell us about the qualities of a great leader, so that I may conform to the design you put forth."

74. The people became silent looking on. The Wayfarer sat in silence for what seemed like an age, then

said, "The worthy do not praise to gain favour, nor self-aggrandize to conflate themselves as an authority. Rather sublime authenticity is the unmistakable mark of their character."

85. Placing a comforting hand upon Makara's shoulder, the Wayfarer continued, "Those who scheme, do so in vain. For the leaders who will arise over you, shall reflect your morals, values, and character - as they are from amongst you. Therefore if you wish to be ruled by fairness and justice, remove from yourselves all traces of corruption and tyranny. If you want to be ruled by generosity and compassion, remove from yourselves all traces of miserliness and indifference. Because replacing a harmful quality with a beneficial one is the way of perfecting all inner qualities; in thought, word and deed.

76. "Those who truly know how to rule are few; for they are those who comprehend diplomacy, pluralism, and empathy; and adhere to it. They seek neither riches nor power, but rather through the congruence of their heart and soul, they seek to serve all with equity and justice. 77. They are neither apathetic in raising the marginalised and weak, nor reluctant to temper the strong and powerful. 78. They are those who have attained to Divine Intimacy and are

guided by it so that the light of good thought shines through, in all of their dealings. 79. You will find no change in their great qualities; whether in public or secret. 80. Their ambition is not for self-interest, but rather to establish the values of mutual co-operation, for the benefit of all people, and by extension, all life."

81. At these words, Makara's cheeks flushed red, and he took his place seated amongst the people with eyes cast down.

82. The Wayfarer continued, "Any person who interacts with them is inspired by an unquenchable desire to become just like them. Yet they are neither boastful nor aloof, due to the inner light of communion which compels them toward the guardianship of all who are in need. Sincere humility pervades their entire being like a beautiful fragrance, so any who may try to crush them, only become marked with the scent of their inner beauty."

83. The Wayfarer then stopped and looking at Makara, said, "Blush not for past inequities, whilst your heart is being washed in the waters of ablution, flowing from the light of divine communion. Rather sit in silence, emptying yourself of all else but the divine light, and be filled with the radiant qualities of all goodness.

84. "Indeed, I have come to sit as a purifier and refiner of gold and silver. I shall sit and refine with the fire of divine rapture, and I shall purify all with the waters of Good Thought.

"Know then, that it is hard for those who do not surrender to Divine Love; for all shall assume the body of the cosmos, and shall be dissolved by love within the infinite, unspeakable name of God. This is a fire of torment for those who will not surrender to it, and it is a flower garden of everlasting bliss for those who surrender without hesitation."

CHAPTER 8

THE JUDGES

85. The Judges stood up with pomp and ostentation, casting looks of condemnation upon the people in every direction. From amongst them, Endibat (Discipline) stepped forward like a towering shadow. His movements were commanding and deliberate, his voice deep, husky and commanding. He said, "Wayfarer, tell us of the rule of law and the punishment of criminals."

86. The Wayfarer replied, "Justice is the root upon which civilisations flourish. It is the fertile soil in which all can safely thrive. Be vigilant in upholding justice; for its absence is the signal of an imminent and tumultuous decline.

87. "Be careful not to conflate justice with the rule of law; for the rule of law can be either just or unjust. Indeed, every person must adhere to just laws; yet every person equally must disobey unjust laws - so that they may not co-

operate with evil. I tell you; it is better to be defeated upholding justice than to triumph by being unjust. So be diligent in the undertaking of your affairs.

88. "Know that the twisting of language for the means of deception can never remove Mankind's innate sovereignty. For that which the Divine Sovereign has granted to humankind can never be removed by any other. So know that if the language of deception is used in court, or upon the paper of a contract, then it is not accepted; for the deceivers have only condemned themselves."

89. At this, Endibat's legs almost weakened beneath him and tears quickly soaked his beard as he stood staring at the Wayfarer, with his hands held over his heart.

90. The Wayfarer continued, "Those who have attained gnosis are guided by a natural disposition, which is in harmony with all goodness – in this state, the right becomes innately clear from the wrong. To the ignorant, it may seem as if such a person is misguided; for they may contradict convention, custom and the interpretation of the law. However, due to the clarity of perpetual communion with The Divine Source, they no longer adhere to doctrine or tradition, but rather act beautifully due to their adherence to justice and goodness alone.

91. "The purpose of law should be to establish and maintain enlightened justice; so the lawmakers should be diligent not to overstep the bounds. If the law is created solely to eliminate harm, its proximity to oppression makes its implementation precarious; therefore, extreme care should be taken to balance the restriction of harm with the freedom to choose.

"Law established for the maintenance of power is called tyranny; it is the shackle of oppression and the desecration of justice - the desperate measure of failed governance. It must be opposed.

92. "When passing judgments; favour mercy, as the letter of the law must be balanced with wisdom, against justice and circumstance. In the case of the powerless, err toward leniency, as their hand may be forced. In the case of the powerful, err towards stringency, as they may use their position to avoid a consequence.

93. "Sentences based upon justice should not inflict retribution; but rather elicit atonement, rehabilitation, and sincere repentance. 94. Do not consider a person who has committed a crime a criminal, instead deem the action that they have undertaken as a criminal act. Just as all innocent

people must be protected, so too all who are guilty are capable of sincere repentance and rectification.

95. "All I have said regarding the external law can also apply to self-rectification and the beautification of good character. For what is outside of you, is also inside of you, and for that which you think, you should hold yourself to account and transform. Therefore practice meditation so that you may be discerning, filling your mind with Divine Light and Good Thought."

96, "Endibat looked softly into the Wayfarer's eyes and said, "I thank you with utmost sincerity for these enlightened words. I am in a state of wonder at how you have condensed such extensive guidance, into such a brief dialogue. I have become filled with a light that I must ponder over, and there is much I must grasp with great urgency - for the sake of all who are brought before me to be judged." And with this, the judges sat down, in a state of sincere humility before the people.

CHAPTER 9

THE YOUNG MAIDENS

97. The young maidens stood up, laughing and blushing, goading each other to speak. Finally, a young maiden from amongst them named Shahwa (Desire) spoke saying, "Tell us about the fulfilment of physical desires."

98. The Wayfarer smiled and said, "The root of desire is in the lower incarnate soul that seeks to reunite with the higher infinite soul. For this is the source of all bliss. As the incarnate soul has come from the realm of endless bliss, it seeks pleasure, and union as a path of return. 99. The infinite soul experiences the joy of union through being effaced in The Divine. However, within the flesh, satisfaction is attained through a physical union, for the fulfilment of physical needs - this confuses the incarnate soul.

100. "Therefore, a new method of distinguishing the correct path to The Divine Essence must be found. You

must achieve this undertaking by forming an intention: That you will only receive, for the pleasure of The Divine Bestower - not solely for the fulfilment of bodily desire. This intention is vitally important; for even in the state of gnosis, the body still demands the satisfaction of its primal needs, which is not damaging in and of itself but can become so. 101. Once you form this intention, the soul can distinguish the origin of pleasures. Thus whereas fornication relieves the bodily need, and gratifies the flesh; marital relations bring together two parts of a single soul, bound to each other through commitment and love. Ascending toward the Divine Source. Their union is not just the meeting of their flesh, but also the meeting of their beings, their love, their trust, their commitment, and their consciousness.

102. "Know that there is a difference between distinguishing origins of pleasures and the self-restraint to choose between them. When the incarnate soul is within the flesh, it is like a rider upon a lion or an unbroken stallion. It takes the utmost strength and will of the rider to submit such a creature to one's commands. 103. At first, the animal resists and throwing the rider to the ground; they are consumed by the lion or trampled by the stallion. However,

over time, by immersing oneself in the Divine Light, such beasts are pacified and naturally begin to conform to the will of the rider.

104. "Choosing to only receive for The Divine Bestower, is a choice to take responsibility, and to sacrifice the part of oneself that is irresponsible. 105. Taking responsibility is a great stage in the incarnation of the soul – it gives one a great strength of will, and clarifies many clouding thoughts from the mind."

106. Shahwa said, "What you have explained to us is a profound teaching. However, if our desires are strong; commanding us to forbidden pleasures – we may be overcome!" She then asked, "Should we overcome our desires first before we attain Gnosis?"

107. The Wayfarer answered, "You speak of desire as if it is a chain binding you to one thing or another. However, this is the illusion of desire. Desire is a searching force of wanting, which flits from one thing to another like a ravenous flame. It does not stay fixed upon one thing; as it is searching for bliss and connection to the Divine Source. Therefore desire can be moved with your will and attention, from one thing to another. So focus with all of

your being upon The Divine Light of Rapture, and enter the realms of eternal bliss."

108. Blushing, Shahwa solemnly said, "I swear we shall do as you have said!" The young maidens then sat down and became immersed in meditation.

CHAPTER 10

THE GREAT WARRIOR

109. As the feast continued, the renowned warrior Qawiy (Strength) stood up, walked close to the Wayfarer, and said, "Tell us about the glory of war, and the great station of the warriors and martyrs!"

110. The Wayfarer embraced him and said, "Be comforted by Divine Love and the outpouring of Divine Care, for I know you have borne the horrors of war while protecting your folk."

Suddenly overcome by the Wayfarer's empathy and with a look upon his face as if he was shocked at his own welling emotions, Qawiy wept uncontrollably. The tears released the trauma of war from his heart.

The people were astounded and began to whisper all around. "What has happened to Qawiy?" said a young man to his father, "Never have we seen him weep!" said a mother to her daughter.

111. The Wayfarer continued, "There is no glory in war, only harm, and great suffering - So know the battle is only won when all fighting has ceased. Glory is attained by those who establish peace, harmony, and justice - So work to these ends so that that glory may be yours.

112. "Know that those who fight against you are not your real enemy; for your enemy is the belief that warfare can be justified. There shall come a day soon, when war is not remembered, except when teaching your youth about a less enlightened age. 113. Therefore you must work every day to protect the sanctity of life and the helpless; for when war becomes unavoidable, the true battle is already lost.

"Sincerely, I say to you, spread close bonds of fraternity amongst yourselves and all people; raising high the ideals of sincere empathy, enlightened dialogue, self-restraint, and peaceful conduct.

114. "The true warriors are those who mediate peace between two adversaries, advocating justice and support for the weak. They are guardians of nature, whose illumined foresight stretches to all future generations. They are the mothers of nations and fathers of generations, whose enlightened teachings shall nurture harmony in the children of humankind.

115. "So I say: Come forth as great warriors of harmony and justice! For the new dawn is emerging on the horizon of consciousness. 116. Let your hearts fill with divine light, like the first rays of daybreak, and let your words become like birdsong; awakening all minds.

117. "As for those you call martyrs, they are those who have died protecting the helpless. They have given the ultimate sacrifice and attained a blessed station. Honour them in a manner that does not glorify the tragedy which claimed them; by working to establish harmony and justice in all lands. Yet while honouring them remember: Those who succeed in mediating peace have a greater station; for they have preserved life, harmony, peace, and justice.

118. "The true martyrs are those who have effaced themselves in The Unspeakable Essence - their station is the bliss of Divine Rapture. Greater still are those who once effaced, realise the unity of being, becoming the cosmos - rectifying the world through the light of Good Thought.

119. "So I say to you: Let the light of gnosis arise in your heart, so that you may efface yourself in inner communion."

120. Qawiy now sat crossed legged in silence. He looked up and said, "My burdens have been relieved, and

my misconceptions have been corrected. As you spoke, my being became filled with Divine Light, and now my mind comprehends the totality of my being – for I have become all that my mind touches."

The Wayfarer replied, "Indeed, it is so."

CHAPTER 11

THE ARRIVAL OF THE KING

121. In a sudden and majestic cacophony of noise, trumpets sounded from the upper entrance to the square. A troop, carrying red banners embroidered with golden lions marched towards the Wayfarer. The gathering parted like a wheel, speeding through a shallow pool. Then, in came the litter of the king, carried by twelve attendants. The troop marched around like a pride surrounding its prey. They moved forward with the litter - placing it upon the ground in front of the Wayfarer, two feet away or closer. An attendant opened the curtains, and the king stepped forth.

122. The people bowed in unison and continued to bow low. No one dared to look up, not even one soul – except for the Wayfarer who sat unmoved and smiling, cross-legged in the middle of the crowd.

123 " Stranger!" Said the advisor of the King, "The King has granted you an audience, so that we may test this

moment and ascertain its worth. Then maybe you will come to know each other's motives!"

The Wayfarer looked into the eyes of the King and said, "Dear child, none are barred from seeking an audience with me - neither beggar nor rulers of men. As for this moment, it is like the opening of the eye of the heart, and the reading of the book of existence; its worth shall manifest with unshakable certainty, and all who read shall be humbled with awe.

"As for my motive, it is to reach the temple of man and to glorify therein the unspeakable name of God. Upon my ascent, I shall gather with me every man, woman and child; unlocking their hearts with the keys of divine communion."

124. The King's cheeks flushed with redness. His advisor quickly stood between the two and said, "Dear Stranger, it appears that the people are quite enamoured with you, and you have clearly garnered their support. Indeed you are eloquent in speech for one unknown to these lands. Yet, even so, you speak in terms that are quite unfamiliar. However fear not, I will forgive your ignorance; for this is not merely a ruler of men, but his royal highness the King! This entire kingdom is under his dominion!

"Now, that you have outlined your motives, as long as it is the truth, it is agreeable. Therefore the King will allow you entry to the Temple of Man, and will escort you there himself! However, if your actions prove that your motives are to rise against us, he will not hesitate to exact his judgement against you!"

125. Moving into the sight of the king, the Wayfarer responded, "Do not fear me in regards to your status or your safety. I have come to set all people free, from a greater tyranny."

The Wayfarer swiftly stood up and stepped toward the King. The royal guards leapt between them with swords ready to strike. The King jumped back into his litter like a timid kitten.

126. The Wayfarer then knelt with hands outstretched and said, "You have thought me ignorant of your station, but I tell you, I see with great clarity, that which others are blind to see. You are a babe, burdened with the responsibilities and finery of a King; a child who fears to walk through his kingdom without a troop of guards. The people wear worn clothes and tire their bodies until death claims them like a scythe reaping dried wheat. Yet you live

in secluded luxury, alone with none but ambitious advisers, attendants and guards as playmates.

"You long for acceptance but fear rejection. You long for freedom but fear assassination or treason. So you hide behind towering walls, not knowing that your greatest enemies have locked themselves in with you; incessantly whispering into your ear night and day."

127. The King's advisor responded, "How dare you! What is your name? You have no authority to be heard here!"

The Wayfarer was utterly unmoved by this outburst and calmly responded, "No name, no word, and no action can take away the innate sovereignty of all humankind; for it is granted through vice-regency to the Sublime Source. What you call me, only reflects your own condition, as my reality is one that names cannot defile."

The advisor of the King shouted, "Guards seize this person!"

But as soon as his words ended, a soft and timid voice came forth from the litter, "Wayfarer… What you have said is true. You have spoken with such insight, that it is as if you have seen through the walls of my palace. Tell me, who are you who says these things?"

128. The Wayfarer said, "I am the herald of the Sovereign of All Creation; who is never absent from Its people, not even for the twinkling of an eye; who gives to them freely, whatever they, with intent, hold within their thoughts. Who suffers with them, while raising them all to the most praised station of direct communion. As they bask in Its light, suffering flees from them like darkness at the breaking of dawn.

"Indeed, I am Its throne and Its crook; It's flail and the jewel of Its crown. I am the intonation of Its word, and the light of Its breath exhaled. O child of this city! I have not come to harm you, as your advisors suggested to you, whilst you remained in the darkened towers of your keep. Rather, I have come to set you free, and to raise you into perfect illumination, along with the people who you serve."

129. The King replied, "Dear Wayfarer, I am bewildered by you, and I fear I have been misguided by my advisors. Let us walk together and talk so that I might receive some of your blessed wisdom!"

130. The Wayfarer said, "Indeed, every voice that offers advice, except for the heart in gnosis, offers a varying degree of misguidance; for true guidance by its nature cannot be conveyed by words - it can only be known

directly within the heart. 131. Those voices which guide to inner communion and goodness are the closest to guidance, and those that speak of harm, egotism and worldly absorption are the whisperers of deep misguidance. So I will expound for you that which is good for you. However, if you would surrender your heart to the light of gnosis, a wisdom that cannot be uttered by lips would instantaneously be yours."

132. Turning toward the upper entrance of the square the Wayfarer said to the King, "Let us walk", at which the entire gathering all stood up to walk with them.

133. The King asked, "Wayfarer, what qualities are required by a King?" The Wayfarer answered, "If I tell you the qualities of a King, you shall assume that claiming kingship is righteous. So I tell you, there is no King other than The Divine Sovereign, the source of the all.

"Each of Mankind holds within their ultimate destiny, the attainment of the state of vice-regency. This state blooms like a fragrant bud, through the realisation of gnosis. They are those who make the inside like the outside, and the outside like the inside, comprehending that all is mind.

134. "By uniting the inner mind, with the outer mind, they cast off the clothing of individuation; once more taking upon themselves the body of the cosmos, becoming the all while living in the flesh. Indeed, humankind has forgotten their vice-regency and their responsibility – given to the universal self and first humans. Therefore they must awaken to the Divine Source - and themselves."

135. Then looking down and smiling at the King, the Wayfarer said, "What you ask me about, are the perfect qualities of the rulers of humanity – and as you have asked, I will tell you:

136. "They have realised their vice-regency and bathed in the light of Divine Gnosis. They peacefully surrender their hearts to The Divine, taking upon themselves all of the attributes of perfection, washing away every harmful trait in the light of Unbounded Love.

137. "They recognise themselves to be the servants of their people, and sincerely humble themselves before all beings. They are never haughty; recognising that each person is either their student or their teacher – never assuming to know which of the two is before them. They are wellsprings of empathy and compassion. They are the flag bearers of justice and fairness. 138. The hammer of

their judgement is forgiveness. The measure of their punishment is nurturing kindness. They are enlightened guides and guide to illumination. They establish the values of mutual co-operation, helping by the work of their own hands, to uplift the conditions of life for all."

139. The King said, "Wayfarer, these things you say seem unobtainable, there is no-one like this in the entire earth!"

Placing his hand upon the King's shoulder, the Wayfarer said, "You have failed to see your own reflection, because of the dust within your eyes. Therefore clean your eyes with the waters of Good Thought, and by the driving force of pure intention, climb to the highest peaks of attainment. For if you yourself will not become as I have described, then who would you wish to do so in your place?"

140. The King ordered his chief advisor Waswasi (Whisperer) to take off the green velvet cloak of his office. Then placed it over the shoulders of the Wayfarer. Its golden tufts glimmered in the light of the sun.

The King had an air of concern and uneasiness about him, he said, "Please advise me. The people complain about paying taxes, what should I do?"

The Wayfarer spoke in a calm and comforting voice saying, "The revenue of taxes should be used for the benefit of all people; beginning with the most in need. Taxes should never be taken to provide luxury to the ruler; rather, the ruler should only take payment equivalent to that which is given to the poorest people in society. However, even though taxes are required to administer the kingdom, and to provide for those in need, the enacting of mutual co-operation between all people should be raised as the highest value in society."

141. The King responded, "Dear Wayfarer, I truly lack knowledge. What is this mutual co-operation you speak of?"

The Wayfarer answered, "It is to work for the benefit of all life and to never impede benefit in thought, word or deed. Do you not see that the river flows by the route of least resistance, but when the flow is stopped the water stagnates? Wealth, riches and resources also flow by the route of least resistance; yet if it is withheld and accumulated, it too begins to stagnate. 142. The stagnation of water causes diseases to arise from it; as does the accumulation of wealth, riches and resources. When the madness of accumulation overtakes the mind, the fear of loss fills the heart, stifling compassion and love. 143. Therefore let wealth, riches and resources flow like a river; knowing that the measure of worldly success is not based upon how much you have, but rather upon the degree to which you relieve suffering, improve conditions and engender strong relationships for all living beings; in thought, word and deed. That is the way of mutual co-operation."

144. As they finished talking, the King and the Wayfarer passed through the upper gate of the square, which was crowned with the carvings of two turtles, and the stone walls of its stairway curved downwards like the pincers of a giant crab. Once they had ascended the stairs, they entered an echoing colonnade. Just within the arch of the gates, the poets were gathered. There they had been looking out upon the square, listening to the words of the Wayfarer, awaiting their time to speak.

CHAPTER 12

THE POETS

145. As the Wayfarer approached, the voices of the poets arose into the air with grace and beautified tones. They came forward as if floating towards the moving crowd. They stopped before the Wayfarer, some kneeling on one knee, some leaning forward attentively.

Their leader Habba (Love) spoke in a voice full of melody and rhythm, saying, "O Wayfarer, we submit ourselves humbly before you, for your words are profound and have become beloved to us all. We request that you teach all gathered here about love and romance."

146. As they leaned in close, the Wayfarer began to speak, saying, "True romance is the effect of love manifesting upon the limbs. How beautifully the lover acts in the presence of the beloved! At first sight, the heart is emancipated by bliss, annihilated in the eyes of the one now adored. From the first glance, thoughts, words, and

actions become perfected, refined and beautified as they are baptized in love.

147. "Therefore, fall in love with The Eternal One, called by the most beautiful names, yet whose name, in reality, cannot be uttered - even by the lovers who draw near.

148. "Love all as yourself, for I tell you; it is so. Empty yourself of yourself, so that you may be filled with The Most Beloved."

149. Habba said, "We are filled! We are filled! Your words have raised us like the wings of angels, into the heights of heavenly domains. O Wayfarer, tell us about the love between a woman and a man, never shall we tire of listening!"

150. The Wayfarer smiled and said, "Now your heart is becoming filled with The Unspeakable Light – Supreme, Divine! The light arises in you, even as these words progress. The heart opens to gnosis, like a bud in flower; witnessing The Unspeakable One, that no words can begin to utter."

151. With closed eyes, the Poets and the people bent down their heads; caught in the ecstatic bliss of gnosis.

152. The Wayfarer continued, "As for love, it has many depths, but no limits; like an ocean with no shores. Such an ocean becomes darker in seven layers - each depth becomes more mysterious than the previous.

153. "The man and the woman in love are like clay and water. Love moulds one into the other, causing one to contain the other, one to become lost in the other; for clay in the hands of love is formed into a cup, and water in the hands of love is poured within, completely taking the form of the cup.

154. "Love is a fire of bliss; so kindle bliss within your loved one. Be gentle and kind, caring and faithful; seek ways to serve one another, and in intimacy, surrender.

155. "Let your love give birth to goodness, beauty, and passion. Through it be respectful, restrained and be bold. 156. Allow it to intoxicate you so that you become lost to the world, and allow it to sober you so that you find yourself in the eyes of your true love."

At this, the poets looked faint and overcome; holding their hands over their hearts or forearms over their foreheads.

The Wayfarer asked, "Has this sufficed you?" Habba replied, "Your words are truly sublime, and our hearts are overcome, have mercy on us!"

The Wayfarer embraced Habba, then stepped forward, walking on toward the temple of man. The poets joined the crowd, following closely behind.

CHAPTER 13

THE GNOSIS OF THE KING

157.   As they walked in the direction of the observatory the King asked, "O Wayfarer if my right hand gives too much mercy, I fear my people will become lazy and rebellious. Yet if my left hand is too austere, I fear my people will continue to suffer, and then to rebel against me. I foresee that whatever I do, I face a great calamity; so please advise me!"

158. The Wayfarer said, "Fear not, and replace a fearful thought with a blessed one, so that you may transform the cause, and attain success. Change begins within the heart before its result manifests within the world. Take the straight path between your two hands. It is the fastest way to the Divine Source, for it fulfils the Divine Will with beauty and perfection."

159. The King asked, "What is the path between my two hands?" Looking at his palms, slightly confused.

The Wayfarer, softly took the King's hands and placed the palms together at the level of his heart, then said, "It is the path which leads through the heart, which quenches the fire of earthly desires with the waters of Divine Love, and leads to the spacious heavens of deep contemplation. It is Good Thought and right action; so give to all in need, and raise all who have stumbled or fallen.

160. "Teach the way of mutual co-operation so that when your people are weak, you shall raise them, and when they are strong, it may be that they too will carry you. 161. By this way, foster love between all of humankind, and leave none in a state of suffering."

162. The King asked, "Wayfarer, I know of many who have vast riches, yet they are full of melancholy and sadness, then surely relieving material needs cannot alleviate the suffering of those that it is destined for?"

163. The Wayfarer responded, "Have you not heard, that only in the communion of gnosis does the heart find rest?

164. "Yet I say to you, work with your influence, wealth, and with your own hands, taking any good action within your power, to alleviate the physical suffering of those in need.

165. "Break open your heart with empathy and compassion. Empty it of judgement completely. Empty it of what you have been told, and learned, and believed. Then in the silence of stillness, allow…"

166. The Wayfarer stopped mid-speech and then turning to the entire crowd continued, "O people! Allow the light of Unspeakable Divine Oneness, to arise within you; for who, in the perpetual gnosis of divine communion, shall know suffering? No! I swear by The Source of all, when divine gnosis awakens within you, suffering shall flee from you, like a startled flock of birds."

167. Turning back to the King, the Wayfarer said, "So I tell you, as the light arises within you now, let it shine forth into the heart of every sentient being; so that you may attain the perfection of the world, through gnosis and Good Thought."

168. The King grabbed hold of the Wayfarer's garments as his knees buckled beneath him, weeping, he said, "The light! The light! O what have I done to my people? O you, Unspeakable Light, forgive me for every thought, word and action that I have ever brought forth into this world. Wash me clean of my ignorance, for I did not know!"

The Wayfarer picked up the young King, as he wept; comforting him at length with such heartfelt compassion that the people of the thronging crowd were deeply moved. Once the King had calmed his sorrow and composed himself in the overflowing peace he beheld, the Wayfarer and the King slowly walked on, in the direction of the observatory, with the people following in crowds behind them.

CHAPTER 14

THE ARISTOCRACY

169. As the Wayfarer walked toward the end of the colonnade, in the direction of the observatory, followed by the swarming crowd, the aristocrats from the city heights stomped down the steps of the high peaks like migrating bison.

The nobleman Shuh (Stinginess) was the first to reach the Wayfarer, bellowing like a snorting bull, "The Wayfarer! Where is the Wayfarer?"

170. As he approached, he saw the green and gold tufted cloak of the chief adviser and the young King walking by the Wayfarer's side. He involuntarily gasped, waving his hand behind his back, signalling for the other aristocrats to stay back.

He then spoke once more; now using an eloquent and noble tone, "Your majesty! Dear Wayfarer! I must apologise! I heard about your delightful gathering;

however, I was unfortunately waylaid by a frightfully important matter!"

Looking at the Wayfarer from head to toe, whilst taking a painfully dry gulp, Shuh continued, "I must ask, your Majesty: Has your delightful and exotic companion been appointed to a position within your council?"

171. The King replied, "Indeed, you are correct. At least for as long as our companion remains amongst us."

Shuh looked at the Wayfarer patronisingly, and said, "It appears you have been besieged by the rabble! Come with me and the nobles of this fine city, and we shall shelter you from the rougher elements. I will make you a guest within my home, where we shall eat the finest foods, surrounded by the most beautiful views, and listening to fine music."

172. The Wayfarer replied, "I thank you Shuh, however, I must decline. Your hospitality is admirable, but your perception is incorrect. A rabble has not besieged me, but rather I am accompanied by the multitude of sincere hearted folk whilst on my journey to the temple of man. As you have invited me, to the exclusion of these good people, who you find contemptible, I must respectfully decline

your invitation; for if I were to accept your invitation, I would validate your disdain for them."

173. Shuh's cheeks flushed with redness and the vein on the left side of his forehead throbbed as if it was ready to burst. He said, "Dear Wayfarer, let us not be overly hasty! Of course, these are sincere people! However, I simply wish to extend the hand of nobility to you on behalf of myself and my associates. Would it not benefit us both to have a private gathering, in which we could discuss some of the more secret and refined matters of life?"

174. The Wayfarer, again declined, saying, "The refined matters are for those who have been refined by the light of gnosis, and the secret matters are for those who understand the signs beyond speech - those who have reached the threshold of that which is comprehensible."

Then raising the right hand to the forehead with the index finger pressed against the thumb, the Wayfarer flicked the index finger, pointing upwards. 175. Shuh looked up confused as all he saw was clear skies.

The Wayfarer continued, "The noble are those who give all, save that which they need to sustain themselves, and who love kindness and justice more than they love the fulfilment of their desires. They are outpouring pitchers, filled with loving care, who exhaust themselves for the service of all – without judgement. If you know of such people, bring them to me!"

176. Shuh replied, "I mean no disrespect, but how can you conflate ascetics with nobles of noble blood? We could never give away our wealth, and why should we? No! We are the guardians of wealth, culture and high society. Without us, everything would decay into disarray!"

177. "Dear Shuh!" The Wayfarer replied, "Blood does not carry nobility; rather, nobility is the fruition of perfected character. Lineage does not pass nobility from one generation to the next; it is inspired through radiant exemplars, to those who sincerely seek to perfect their inner selves. Therefore do not rely upon blood and wealth when gnosis raises you before the Source of all existence; for if you rise before Its brilliance as a wretch, you will burn in the fires of regret, having awakened to the bare truth of your being. Seek then the good, leaving behind all wretchedness, so that you may shine forth as a lantern of goodness."

178. Shuh groaned a pompous groan and then said, "Indeed, your words are very flowery, and the mob is enthused by the prospect of being raised to our stature. But

Wayfarer, these uneducated folk do not have the intellects to know what is best for them – I appeal to you to use reason! Is a lion like a dormouse? Is an eagle like a lowly snake? No! That is foolishness for simple-minded folk. We have heard enough; we shall be on our way!"

179. The Wayfarer called after the Shuh and the aristocrats, saying, "Before you leave, will you not listen to a few parting words…"

Shuh stopped and turned to reply, "We have many pressing matters, but I will humour you again - please make your point as brief as possible!"

180. The Wayfarer spoke, saying, "Indeed a lion is not like a dormouse and an eagle is not like a lowly snake, but the destiny of Mankind is to unite the two within their single being: The strong and the meek, the high and the low, the earthly and the infinite soul."

181. This reply caught hold of something in Shuh, or rather, it was like it planted something within him. At first, it manifested as curiosity, but in truth, it was something much more profound. He stood with an astonished look upon his face, feeling something inside; something he had never felt before. He said, "Continue; please speak on…"

182. The Wayfarer continued, "Indeed, mankind is one body, one mind and one soul, so whoever harms their brother or sister, has truly only harmed themselves."

Shuh reeled at these words as if they had cut him deep inside. The harm he felt was that of a fissure forming in the solidity of his pride-filled heart. 183. The light, which glanced through this crack, compelled his lips before he could even think, "how can this be so? Do you think I am like these uncultured folk?"

The Wayfarer said, "Indeed you are not *like* these folk, you are one and the same - yet you see it not. 184. However, when gnosis arises within you, you will come to know.

"I tell you: This world is an unrefined ore, awaiting its purification into gold; so woe to the one who does not undertake this great task of purification.

"The world before you is like liquid mercury, taking the shape of every vessel that contains it, reflecting everything that is displayed before it. So ponder that which you display within yourself and correct that which you do not wish to see manifest before your face."

185. Painfully Shuh replied, "I am not like these vagabonds! How can I accept this!"

The Wayfarer lovingly said, "Do not hate the reflection, yet curse the mirror. Instead, smile and see the mirror smile at you!

"O Shuh, the people are not impoverished and suffering due to *their* inadequacies, but rather due to the actions of your own two hands. 186. The aristocrats have come like wolves to fleece these gentle sheep. Then you blame them for suffering due to their lack of wool. I say to you, find within yourself that place, where your disdain for them rests, then transform it into empathy and care like a metalsmith, making a lofty crown from a lowly ore. 187. When you do this, you will see a great transformation manifesting before your own eyes, and you shall know with certainty that the Unspeakable Source is capable of all things."

188. Shuh raised one eyebrow with an air of disbelief and said, "If God is capable of all things, why is there suffering, pain and loss?"

Without hesitation, the Wayfarer replied, "All things flow outward from the Divine Source. Then by Its power and will; it flows through the soul and heart of Man. Each thought of the heart and mind restricts, lets flow, directs and manifests; yet Mankind is asleep to their purpose.

189. "The Unspeakable One created Mankind as an intricately veiled mystery, to be the conductor of the symphony of life. Yet Mankind has fallen into the darkness of ignorance and forgetfulness; so this symphony has descended into chaos.

"Mankind has become accustomed to attributing the cause of every feeling of suffering to God while claiming the origin of every success for themselves. In reality, the Limitless Bestower gave them the world and made them the vice-regents of it. Therefore, it is in accordance with their habitual thoughts that The Divine brings forth the conditions of abundance or suffering."

190. Shuh remained silent for some time, no longer feeling so self-righteous and smug. He then said, "If what you have said is true, then we have become *truly* lost. How can you prove what you say?"

The Wayfarer answered, saying, "In your heart, find your enemy, and transform your hate for them into love. Then you shall also see their hate transform into love for you."

Shuh said, "This is too difficult. I could never do it!"

The Wayfarer responded, "Then give to the poor from your own hands. Raise the weak by your own arms and help them walk. Then you will see how they respond to you."

Shuh said, "O Wayfarer, this would be incredibly hard for us, as we have not yet been accustomed to humbling ourselves, nor are we accustomed to giving to the poor. Either tell us something else we can do to prove your words to us, or we shall depart from you."

Undeterred by Shuh's stubbornness, the Wayfarer replied, "Smile at each person you see; greet them with beautiful words, then come and tell me what response you have found? In this simple act, you will see that that which pours forth through your heart and mind, is reflected to you upon the mirror of the world. 191. In this is a great secret; for wherever you turn, there is the face of the Unspeakable Majesty."

At this, Shuh sighed, and along with the aristocrats, he turned and left.

192. The King then turned to the Wayfarer, saying, "I feared that they would be too haughty to accept your message!"

The Wayfarer frowned and said, "And so, as you conceived it, it came to pass. Therefore, you must change what is within you concerning them. As for me; I see their course with certainty - it shall be true and unfailing."

CHAPTER 15

THE ASTRONOMERS

193. The great multitude reached the level of the observatory, on route to the temple of man. The Wayfarer stopped to rest. The King also rested as the crowd thronged around them. As the people slowly assembled and began to sit down, the astronomers Basrara (Vision) and Dina (Inner Sight) emerged from within the observatory. 194. The two were elderly, walking with sticks. Their long beards almost trailed upon the ground.

As they approached the Wayfarer, Dina said, "We were aware of your coming, and knowing that you would pass this way we have awaited you. We are stargazers, Astronomers, spending our time looking at the sky, reading its signs and watching its motions."

Basara then said, "Tell us about the heavens above us. Do the stars hold power? Do the planets dictate our fate?"

195. The Wayfarer replied, "The heavenly bodies above us are akin to a timepiece, and a book. They are an intricate clock, and a scripture, written with the pen of starlight, upon the far horizons; read by those who know the language of signs. 196. The stars do not dictate the fate of Mankind. But those who deny that the heavenly bodies have been granted power, need only stand in the heat of the day and contemplate the sun. Just as the sun signals the coming of the day, causing us to wake, and also signals the changing of the seasons, showing us when to plant our seed or when to reap the harvest, so too all other heavenly bodies exert a force and indicate the many great cycles of life within the cosmos. 197. From the germination of intricate influences to the rooting of potential outcomes; from the budding of Mankind's emotions to the blossoming of Mankind's consciousness. Everything is elaborately indicated by the signs inscribed within the heavens and within you; all by the power of the Divine Source."

198. Dina sighed, "Humph!" and said, "I grasp how we may read the signs within the heavens, but I do not grasp how we can read signs within ourselves."

199. The Wayfarer frankly and respectfully replied, "You have spent your long life looking outwards, learning

the science of the stars, yet you are unable to see the same signs within your own heart and soul.

200. "So I say to you: Attain gnosis, so that through inner communion, you will come to see, that what you perceive as outside of yourself; from your flesh to the farthest limit of your vision, is projected outward through your own heart, like the patterns of a blazing lamp, shining forth from the Divine Luminosity."

201. Basara spoke saying, "You say the heavenly bodies do not dictate our fate, yet we have studied the peculiarities of their effects, so we have seen the fate of mankind tied to the stars!"

202. The Wayfarer responded, "O Basara! Do not confuse an influence or effect, with an unchangeable fate! Indeed, the sun rises and brings forth light each day, and the creation flourishes with life; and when it is dark, Mankind naturally feels the effects of tiredness. However, Man may sleep through the day and stay awake throughout the night. So too, the other heavenly bodies exert particular effects; but they do not bind an individual to a specific outcome.

203. "Take the elements as an example: Amongst many other effects: Fire can warm, yet it can also burn;

water can quench the thirst, or it can overwhelm and drown; earth can consume the dead or nurture the new life of a seed, and air can become a destructive gale or carry the slowly drifting birds unto unseen heights. 204. All effects are only apparent and are only tied to causes by habitual nature. All things originate from the Divine Source, Unspeakable and Unspoken, and none other. Yet that source has made Mankind responsible for the effects which they cause.

205. "Therefore, wake up, O Mankind! Wake up to your true self, for when the light of gnosis anoints you, and when the outer and inner are married as one, you shall realise the unity of the self as the entire cosmos. 206. Then if you truly believe; whatever you hold within your heart and mind will begin to manifest before you. So turn your attention within, rectifying the negative and habitual thoughts regarding the world, which you habitually recall into being. 207. Replace every negative thought with good thoughts, and you will transform the entire world. Know then, that all of this shall happen by the will of the Supreme Source, Disposer of All Affairs."

208. Basara sat down on a low wall of the observatory gardens and said, "I have studied the stars my whole life;

thinking that I knew every facet of this vast knowledge. 209. Now you have come and reasoned with me; correcting my misunderstandings and showing your prowess in this subject. But I am old now, and every movement is a great effort, so please grant me knowledge of a simple act, through which I can attain a greater depth of illumination."

210. The Wayfarer said, "If the moon enters the house of your birth for three days, and you maintain your presence therein; will these nights not shine with the whiteness of illumination amongst the darkness of other nights? Will, you not be illuminated beyond measure therein?"

Basara replied, "Yes, indeed, but how does one maintain oneself in the house of their birth?"

The Wayfarer responded, "Fast therein, sit in meditation and communion, and burn fragrant herbs, glorifying the name of the Unspeakable Majesty; then you shall be filled with light."

211. Basara thanked the Wayfarer profusely. Then Dina spoke again saying, "I too wish for you to grant me knowledge. Tell me how does the cycle of the stars relate to the cycles of Mankind?"

212. The Wayfarer looked deeply and penetratingly into Dina's eyes, to the point he felt as if there was nothing left of the hidden thoughts of his heart.

213. The Wayfarer then spoke saying, "Indeed, you have perceived something of great importance, and you have chanced upon the periphery of a great mystery. You ask a question, yet you already know the answer. 214. How strange it is that you ask me now, something you had asked before, yet when you asked the first time, you knew not the answer, but now, since the instant you saw me approaching upon the distant horizon, you knew the truth as if it were your reflection. 215. O, Dina! The time is not ripe for me to reveal this mystery, yet it is near at hand."

Dina looked at the Wayfarer with a look of wonder and said, "Then, if that mystery is too great, guide us to the gnosis and communion you speak of."

216. The Wayfarer replied, "Rest in the stillness of meditation, rest in the unspeakable name of the Divine Mystery; then as the night of ignorance passes away, the light of gnosis shall rise like the breaking day."

Dina and Basara both closed their eyes as their faces shone with the bliss of communion. The Wayfarer then said in a soft and gentle tone, "It is time to move onward!"

CHAPTER 16

THE PRIESTS

217. Near the doors of the temple, the priests stood with grandeur; walking toward the Wayfarer in groups from several different directions. Each group had its peculiarities and was led by its own leader. The Wayfarer stood at the bottom of the steps as the first of the leaders, Iman (belief), stood at the top of the steps and began to speak.

He said, "Wayfarer, we are the theologians. Tell us about religion and the purity of creed."

218. The Wayfarer responded, "The words of Mankind cannot grasp The Divine Reality. Only through Gnosis; direct communion with The Divine Presence, can Mankind know the reality of God. 219. Those who theorise about it, unintentionally misdirect the people from the Source of All Things; for nothing can contain It, except for the surrendered heart. 220. Therefore I say to you, do not

theorise; rather still your lips and minds so that that gnosis may arise within your hearts.

"As for religion; its essence is the direct path to gnosis. However, in the minds of men, gnosis has been overshadowed by tradition and tribalism, so be diligent in taking the path to the Divine, rather than the path to tribal acceptance.

221. "In the state of ignorance, the religion itself appears as the ultimate truth. However, when gnosis arises, and you exist in a state of direct communion, the purpose of religion becomes clear from that of the truth of the Sublime Essence. Then the knower of God must choose; surrender to the will of men, or surrender to the Divine Essence in all of its unfathomable and sublime glory. 222. Therefore, in the tradition of the prophets, do not say, "I am of this religion", nor "I am of that religion"; rather say I am of those who peacefully surrender to God, The Source of All Existence."

223. Tahara (purity) then spoke saying, "O Wayfarer! Please tell us about ablution and cleanliness."

The Wayfarer said, "Ablution has two aspects, outer and inner. 224. Inwardly, ablution is to wash in utter humility, in the waters of the Divine Intimacy through meditation. It is to clear the heart and mind of false perceptions, witnessing that all causes and all effects are from The Supreme Source. 225. Outwardly, it is not washing for the sake of dirt removal, even though washing with water accomplishes this task. It is washing away the individuated, self-centred, fleshy persona from the eternal soul, by rubbing the limbs with the lowest substance on earth. So when water is available, the limbs are rubbed with it, as water finds the lowest point upon the earth's surface. But when water is not present, the limbs are rubbed with the earth itself. That is because, in the absence of water, dirt is the lowest substance. 226. Using dirt indicates that the true ablution is deeper than physical washing, as dirt cannot clean the limbs, but by its innate nature, any being that it lays upon becomes humbled."

227. The next to speak was Ibadah (Servitude), who said, "Tell us about prayer and acts of worship."

The Wayfarer responded, "Worship is like a boat, used to cross a great ocean; it is the great conveyance of the soul, taking it to The Divine Source. Its acts engender the peaceful surrender of the entire being to the Unspeakable Sublimity. Take then the journey, and neglect not the conveyance of the soul. 228. Like ablution, worship also has two aspects, outer and inner; for that which is outside of you is also inside of you, and that which is inside of you is outside also. The outer aspect of worship is to surrender the lower, incarnated soul, through the performance of specific actions. 229. The inner aspect of worship is meditation, which leads to communion through the unity of the lower bodily soul and the higher infinite soul.

230. "Meditation is the essence of worship; for it is the open doorway to the Divine Source. Worship devoid of meditation, upon the Divine Essence, is an empty act and a cultural habit devoid of life. Worship which contains meditation upon the Divine Essence is a living act and an expression of the soul within the material realm. 231. That is the path to gnosis, so I tell you; be still and let the light of communion arise within you."

232. Irada (Will) spoke up saying, "Dear Wayfarer, please tell us about fasting and its benefits."

The Wayfarer responded, "Fasting develops inner strength, empathy, compassion and intimacy with the Divine. 233. Fasting from food and water has many benefits; however, it should not be taken to extremes; for the purpose is not to destroy life, but rather to enrich it. Therefore the knowers use reason and common sense to maintain their bodily health, whilst enriching their inner being as their souls ascend into heavenly bliss.

234. That is the fast you have asked me about, and I have explained it in detail. However, I say to you: The greatest fast, is to fast from negative thoughts and from co-operating with evil; such a fast should never be broken. 235. Those seated in the light of gnosis know this from direct experience, for they are perpetually witnesses of The Source of all good.

236. The next to speak was Ya'sa (Striving) who said, "O Wayfarer, please speak to us about pilgrimage."

237. The Wayfarer replied, "The pilgrimage you ask about is the journey of the body to the holy places and the fulfilment of certain rites therein. However, the true pilgrimage is the journey of the soul, seeking enlightenment, gnosis, and effacement in The Divine Essence. 238. The paths of this pilgrimage are meditation and stillness. It is the unification of the outer and the inner. It is a journey, guided by the heavenly stars. It is the transformation of the cosmos within, so that the external cosmos, may be perfected. Thereby, it is ascension through the seven heavens to the supreme throne of The Holy

Mystery. 239. So I say, step forward upon the path O humble pilgrim!"

240. Qurban (Sacrifice) loudly interjected saying, "Tell us about the sacrificial animals offered to God, how many should we offer? What is the reward of the sacrifice?"

241. The Wayfarer responded, "How strange it is, that you *seek* to kill the creatures which God gave life, as an act of worship and in thanksgiving for your own life!"

242. Qurban retorted, "Do you reject that which is written in the scriptures? It is an order of God to sacrifice an animal in Its name!"

243. The Wayfarer said, "Indeed the language of the scriptures is profound and embedded with deep meanings. 244. It is not truly possible to understand the scriptures unless you have attained inner communion; for God is the exegete of its meanings, and therefore this is an expected pre-requisite of the interpreter.

"It is through inner communion with The Sublime Light that all meanings are made clear. 245. So beware of the interpretations of those who have not attained gnosis; for they put forth guesses and conjecture as if it were the ultimate truth, and they interpret from the limited perspective of their own experience and the fluctuating condition of their hearts.

246. "Sincerely, I tell you, the beast of burden that must be sacrificed is the immaturity of your persona, which takes no responsibility for its actions; whilst enjoying every passion of the flesh. 247. It is the individuated, incarnated, bodily conception of self, which is inwardly sacrificed, so that the infinite soul may take upon the primordial, universal body, and effacement in the Divine.

248. "I ask you who cling to the letter of the scripture, to use reason: What benefit does the sacrifice of an animal bring to you or God? You inflict death upon that which God gave life, believing you have fulfilled an obligation. Yet this act is out of harmony with the divine ethics of preserving innocent life, eliminating harm and the preservation of bodily health.

249. The benefit in sacrificing your fleshy nature, however, is that you realise your true self, and the inner and outer unite as the individuated, incarnate soul realises its infinite eternality. 250. The soul and materiality unite in the realisation that all is mind, through which the soul becomes a doorway to The Divine Source. 251. The Divine Outflowing becomes unobstructed by the carnal nature, and

gnosis arises in the heart, as God is realised in the most intimate union. Then, bliss and harmony shine forth from your heart; as if from a dazzling lamp, and the secret name of God is enthroned upon the heart and mind, as perfection is attained."

252. Harfiyah (Literalism) pushed forward and said, "The language of the scripture does not lend itself to this interpretation, and our minds prevent us from the interpretation you give. Anyhow, the meat of the sacrifice is to feed the poor, so how can we reject what is clear, in favour of what is not apparent?" 253. The Wayfarer said, "It is not the scripture which does not lend itself to these interpretations, but rather your hearts and minds. 254. O Harfiyah, know that if the meat of animals had tasted putrid, you, yourself would have found the interpretation I have given. So I say to you, it is not your minds which prevent you from understanding; rather it is your tongues, your noses, and your stomachs.

255. "Earnestly I tell you, God does not curse something you have been ordered to do, nor with which you are commanded to feed the poor. Yet the flesh of animals causes disease and sickness within the body, and the killing of animals afflicts your minds, hearts and souls -

so seek wisdom in enlightened interpretation and do not be fooled by your lustful desires.

256. "Give to the poor and needy whatever you can. Give them good foods, clothing, and shelter; and eliminate poverty through mutual co-operation."

257. Harfiyah responded, saying, "So do you now forbid what the prophets previously have allowed? People in certain circumstances need to kill animals to live – Should they now let themselves die?"

258 The Wayfarer smiled and said, "I have not come to forbid nor to allow. Instead, I have come to unify the shattered shards of one vessel, guiding the people to the intimacy of divine gnosis; so that all things may become apparent to them, within their selves.

259. "It is within your nature and within your right to preserve your lives – but if you must kill to do so; then do so with a heavy heart. 260. I say to you: The situation is dire when there is no option but to kill to survive, and if you kill to eat without need, then your situation is unfathomable. To take the life of a conscious being, even when the need is critical, is a horror. To feast upon such a corpse is a horror of horrors. 261. So take good means to prevent it through preparation, foresight and mutual co-

operation. But if you have no choice except to do so, do not revel in the meal; rather eat with deep remorse; for you are eating the corpse as its funeral, and you yourself have become its grave.

262. "O, people! Eat of the blessed plants, which even once killed give forth their seed, and which from one stalk or one root, a new plant grows, and which after death in winter, return to life again in spring.

263. "The herb of the earth and the fruit of the green tree are akin to the eternal soul; whereas the meat of an animal is the symbol of the incarnated, ignorant soul and the instinctual nature of the flesh. 264. Therefore I say: Sacrifice the individuated self, so that you may become the cosmos – arising into the union of illuminated gnosis."

CHAPTER 17

THE MYSTICS

265. The Wayfarer began to ascend the steps of the temple. From amongst the crowd, the aristocrats approached once more. However, now they had removed their beautiful clothes and jewellery and were wrapped in simple sheets. Shuh and his group smiled at the Wayfarer and bowed their heads out of humble respect.

266. Shuh spoke softly, Asking, "May we accompany you, for we have found in what you guided us to, truth of a sublime nature. We wish to take from you as much benefit as we can?"

The Wayfarer returned a joyful smile, and said, "Merge with the people and separate from your selves. Give way to others before yourself and serve those who are in need of your service. Then you shall have truly accompanied me."

Once more Shuh and the aristocrats smiled. Shuh said, "As you wish!" And the aristocrats separated from each other dispersing amongst the crowd.

The Wayfarer turned back toward the temple and breathing in a deep breath of contentment, walked through the colossal doorway, taking a seat in the centre of the great hall.

267. From the inner sanctum of the temple, an elderly woman slowly approached guided by a young girl. The young girl carried an incense burner, which swung on a long chain and let out thick plumes of deeply scented smoke. Moving in complete silence, she came and sat at the Wayfarer's feet. 268. Then, out of the light of the twelve alcoves of the temple hall, other figures emerged like shadowy silhouettes, approaching in silence. 269. Each person quietly took a seat around the Wayfarer, as the scent of pungent herbs and heavy musk filled the air. The atmosphere was deep and meditative.

270. The elderly woman Sirr (secret) raised her hands and made various symbols with them. The young girl Ayah (sign) spoke in a voice full of sweetness, saying, "This is my grandmother, she says: I am Sirr, an elder from

amongst the mystics, we have been awaiting you for many years, so we welcome you now with love and awe."

271. The Wayfarer and Sirr embraced, tears flowed down Sirr's deeply wrinkled cheeks. After some time, she moved back and continued signing, all the time staring intently into the Wayfarer's eyes.

The Wayfarer nodded as her hands moved, but before Ayah could translate, the mystic known as Ikhlas (sincerity) spoke aloud saying, "I am Ikhlas, and I must be heard! The priests of the temple accuse us and slander us in front of the people; redeem us today, our dear teacher!"

272. The Wayfarer turned to Ikhlas and said, "Dear Ikhlas, who has accused you except for yourself? And who has heard a slander against you but your own ears? For you have looked into a mirror whilst accusing yourself; not recognising your own face; nor what you contain within your own heart. 273. Dear Ikhlas, I tell you, That which is outside of you cannot harm you…"

Then, placing the palm of the right hand on the chest of Ikhlas, the Wayfarer continued, "That which is inside of you, is that which will harm you - until it is transformed into Good Thought. I tell you, truly, when you make the two as one, you shall witness the supreme truth, and the sword which swings to strike you shall evaporate like the phantom of a passing thought. Therefore O Ikhlas, awaken!"

274. Ikhlas groaned in a long and foreboding tone, falling backwards; limp as if death had taken his soul. The people all around caught him and lowered him to the floor. The Wayfarer signalled to give him space, but he lay motionless for such a long time that the people began to fear that he had died.

275. Then, once the people had given up hope for him, he opened his eyes and sat upright. Composed and peaceful, his eyelids heavy upon his eyes, he whispered, "I have been raised to the supreme deity, and filled with its sublime light…"

He then bowed his head shyly and said, "I have no more questions." After which he fell into silence and deep meditation.

276. The Wayfarer turned back to Sirr who began signing with her hands once more. Ayah spoke saying, "What you have said is of such magnitude, it is bewildering, and many have not grasped the realities about which you speak. 277. Explain to us those things we do not yet understand, and that will open the doors of

understanding for all people. What is the nature of this world? And how has it come to exist?"

278. The Wayfarer nodded to Sirr, then raising one finger and making various gestures said, "The world came into existence through the perception of it. This perception is the undulating word, which arose from the Supreme Awareness of the Unspeakable Essence. 279. The Unspeakable Essence proclaimed the word to itself; for there is no other. This proclamation rippled in the Unfathomable Awareness as unbounded imagination; creating a vast spaciousness, known as the pregnant void. 280. As It brought forth the pregnant void, The Light of Supreme Knowing simultaneously shone forth. This light is the outflowing from the Unspeakable Essence, penetrating deeply into the vast spaciousness. 281. The Light of Supreme Knowing burst forth; annihilated in the gnosis of the Unfathomable Essence. This Light inscribed the Divine Command into the pregnant void, like a pen writing the world into existence. 282. It's inscribing was as the arousal of all vibrations; thus, this singular word contained all created being, and from it, all of creation came into existence. The word carried the meaning of "being" and therefore all became.

283. "This union of light and spaciousness is the universal, primordial man. In this state, it exists in perpetual and exalted gnosis of the Unspeakable Essence. The Supreme Essence precedes its being and that of all existence; for time itself issues forth from It. That is the reality of the celestial self, which you shall come to know."

284. The mystic Qudus (Holiness) leant forward, with a shawl hanging over her head so far that it completely covered her face. In a slow and unnerving voice, that sent shivers up the spine, she asked, "Wayfarer... How did the multitude of beings and numerous creations come to be? Why are there many devoid of gnosis, when the divine source created one unified pair, in perpetual gnosis?"

285. The Wayfarer said, "What you ask is of great importance to our affair. So listen with complete comprehension. The primordial man, which is the unified pair, was created by the will to bestow and was created as the will to receive the divine bestowal. The Divine Source exhaled into this being Its soul, which held within it the secret desire of The Sublime Essence to know Itself. Due to this, a longing arose within the primordial man. This longing to know Itself was filled with a great power akin to a sublime version of the intellect, which tore the light and

spaciousness apart in recognition of the differences in their qualities. 286. Like the intellect, this great power sought to separate qualities into increasingly refined elements as a means of knowing each of them. However, the intellect does not comprehend, that if you cut apart a living body, you will inevitably extinguish its life. 287. Therefore, in the same way, as glass shatters under the effect of resonance; at a certain point, this increasing division caused a shattering of the soul in the universal man. From this came the myriad of things, all differing from each other, and all in a varying state of forgetfulness.

"Therefore, universal, primordial consciousness left the paradise of perpetual gnosis. 288. However, when the secret longing within is awakened, and the soul realises its true purpose. Then the heart and mind turn to meditation, the intellect is discarded, and all things return as one in remembrance of their Divine Origin."

289. The next of the mystics to speak was Aintibah (Attention) who said, "I meditate, worship for long hours, and I have spiritual experiences. Tell me what is my station amongst the mystics?"

290. The Wayfarer asked, "Have you arrived at the light of the Divine Presence?"

Aintibah responded, "I have not, but I have had great visions and prophetic dreams. I can read the minds of others and see over great distances."

291. The Wayfarer asked, "You can read the minds of others like an open book, but can you not see the light which is manifest within your own heart?" Aintibah reluctantly replied, "I can not."

The Wayfarer held Aintibah's two hands and asked, "What use are meditations and worship if they do not open you to the light of Divine Communion? What use are spiritual experiences if you have not experienced the bliss of the Divine Presence?"

292. Aintibah lowered his head as the Wayfarer earnestly continued, "I tell you, your station is akin to the money lenders, the traders and the fornicators. Just as they had been completely distracted by the worldly life, so too, you have become completely distracted by the spiritual life. Both you and they look to your achievements as marks of success, not realising that the successful ones are those who attain the precious diamond of indestructible gnosis."

293. Aintibah spoke saying, "Is it not forbidden to contemplate the Divine Essence; for it cannot be known except through the confirmation of belief? Do you guide

people to disobedience rather than the like of what I have received?"

294. The Wayfarer sighed and with a glance of heart-melting compassion said, "I call not to contemplation, for this is the realm of the intellect, which cannot reach the Divine Essence. This is because the intellect dissects as a means of knowing a thing. Yet the Divine Essence is utterly transcendent beyond this; for it is sublime, incomprehensible oneness Itself. Therefore, It is futile to ponder and reflect upon the Divine Essence with the intellect. It can only be known through entering into silence, and by the stilling of thought, through meditation. Then in the deafening stillness, a light manifests within the heart, and the inner eye opens. Through this inner sight, the Sublime Essence is witnessed, and the heart becomes an outflowing of unspeakable Divine Love and a radiant lantern of rapture. O Aintibah! I would guide the people to this, with my last breath, even if the whole of humanity marked me as a blasphemer. For those who have attained gnosis must make a choice: To blaspheme against the intellects of man, by peacefully surrendering to the Divine Essence, or to blaspheme against the Sublime Essence by bowing to the intellects of man."

295. Aintibah asked, "How can Man function in the world if they are in a state beyond intellect?"

296. The Wayfarer said, "The blind could never know that the purpose a mirror is to reflect their image. 297. Rather, all they can say about it is: It is cool to the touch, smooth, shaped and thin. To investigate further, they break the mirror. Once broken, they find that its defining quality is its sharpness and ability to cut. Therefore they use the shards of the mirror as a cutting implement, in their search to know the things around them; separating one quality from another.

298. "A person of gnosis in this example is like a person given vision and comprehension. They are like the rising of the sun in the sky, which dispels the darkness of ignorance. From the state of gnosis, they come to see the reality of the myriad of things as they manifest from the Divine Source; just as they comprehend their reflection in a mirror, and understand its purpose.

299. "Therefore, I say that Man functions in perfection when the mirror is whole and vision is attained. So do not grasp at the broken shards, to cut apart your own body. Rather sit before the mirror and smile; for in the smile is

the manifest light of The Sublime and Compassionate; bestower of all good."

Aintibah closed his eyes remaining in contented silence.

300. The mystic Zuhud (asceticism) sat completely wrapped in a coarse woollen blanket. He was emaciated, with dry, chapped lips and unkempt hair, appearing weak and exhausted. He slowly began to articulate words from his dry mouth, "The ease of what you call to sounds appealing to the masses, indeed it is far more mystical and mysterious than the ascetic practices of self-denial that our masters have taught us. But in truth, reaching such states requires great hardship, as well as many years of asceticism. 301. Some may be blessed with spontaneous realisation, but they are few and far between. For most, it will be a life long struggle, working toward a goal that many will never even achieve: This is not the path for the many; it is the path of the elect. What say you?"

302. Examining Zuhud's weak, fragile form, with eyes filled with pity, the Wayfarer asked, "After everything your masters have made you endure, Have you attained that which they promised you?"

303. Zuhud moved his rough tongue around the inside of his dry mouth with an expression of distaste at the question that had been posed. He slowly responded, "I still have not removed the traces of ego and desire from myself, therefore through my own failing, I have not yet made myself worthy!"

304. The Wayfarer looked at Zuhud with gentility and care then said, "If you have not removed the traces of ego and desire within you when you are in such a dire condition, then you should evaluate the worth of either the method or the goal.

305. "One who would put their disciple through such hardship, harming their health and bringing them to destruction at their own hands, knows nothing of illumination or gnosis.

"Ruining the body is not a spiritual act; neither will it eliminate the traces of ego and desire, until it brings you to the hands of death.

306. "Rather, it is annihilation in the unity of Divine gnosis that washes the ego and desires of all else other than the Sublime Essence."

307. Zuhud wept, but no tears would fall, he said, "I have tried so hard! I have brought myself to the edge of

life, and my desire for food, comfort and pleasure has not left me. My body has pained me, demanding food and water, yet I fear taking too much, for this is what I am known for, this is why the people hold me in high regard!"

308. The Wayfarer asked the people to bring water and food. Zuhud sighed a lifetime of exhaustion from his lungs, then ate and drank whilst crying dry tears.

The Wayfarer then spoke softly saying, "Attaining inner communion and the light of gnosis is neither hard nor does it require great self-deprivation. Those who teach that the light is trapped within the flesh that must be destroyed, neither know what the flesh is nor have they known the light. For the flesh is the illusion of a boundary of the self, and the light cannot possibly become trapped.

309. "Rather, gnosis is the natural state of being, which is present in every creature, though it is completely hidden by the blindness of their fearful, neurotic and whirling thoughts. Gnosis is attained by letting go of thoughts and preconceptions; not in a battle with the flesh or the chatter of the mind, but rather by merely resting in the vast spaciousness and great peace of silence.

310. "O, people! Rest within the unspeakable, unspoken name of the Sublime God - filled with eternal bliss and the light of Divine intimacy."

311. Touching Zuhud on the shoulder, the Wayfarer said "O Zuhud, listen to me now; for it is a great wonder, that when Man hears of this truth, whether they are a poor servant, a king, a priest or a mystic; they resist it - even if it has been their life's work.

312. "So I say, do not restrict that which the Divine Source has made infinitely vast; for that which I guide to, does not take excruciating self-denial, it does not take years of practice, nor is it the property of an elite group; it is available to every being with ease – so stop fighting ease with the superstition of unworthiness and inevitable hardship.

313. "Divine communion is not mysterious and unobtainable; it is a light which clarifies all things. Yet, those who fear it empowering the people, cover and obscure it. They are like one who takes the seed of the tree of life and locks it within an iron chest saying, "This seed will grow from within this chest - if you devote your life to me, and bring your sacrifices to me, and give up your luxuries, your possessions, and your minds to me. 314.

Even then, it will not grow unless you understand its mystery which I hold!" Indeed, that iron chest is incessant thought.

So I say, "Plant the seed in fertile soil, water it, and allow it to grow in the light of the sun!" The fertile soil is silent meditation, the water is peaceful surrender to Divine Love, and the light of the sun is letting go of all preconceptions, so that the light of communion may arise. 315. Yet some still say, "No! This seed *shall* grow within this chest!" For they have come to love the chest, rather than the seed within it."

316. By the time the Wayfarer had finished speaking, many of those gathered nearby, including Aintibah, and Zuhud were weeping.

The Wayfarer continued, "Do not weep O, people! Rather plant the seed of gnosis in fertile soil."

317. Aintibah and all those who wept, calmed themselves, entering into deep meditation. After some time, a heaviness lifted from them, as if the light which began to fill them, permeated the air - dispersing a sweet fragrance like the incense of Sirr.

318. Breaking his meditation, the young mystic Irfan (Gnosis) spoke asking, "O Wayfarer, veiled and beyond the

first light is a more sublime intangible essence; a light, beyond light. It is God, the Divine Source. Expound for the people, a description of God and tell them what the light that veils it is?"

319. The Wayfarer said, "You have asked one of the most important questions, and indeed it can only be answered by Its own Sublime Outpouring; by entering into the communion of your own surrendered heart. But as you have asked, I will say as much as words can contain - even though the reality transcends all words. 320. The first light you have come to, which veils the Sublime Essence, is the light of prophethood. It is the first created light. From it, all great beings, prophets and messengers manifested. The greatest of which manifested through the highest realisation of this light. 321. From this light came all souls, all awareness, and all existence; for indeed it is all one; only appearing as shattered parts due to individuated perception. 322. It shines forth in the great void, like a lamp in a niche. That is the primordial, fully illumined self; the cosmic consciousness, universal Man, the all. 323. Beyond this, veiled by the supreme purity of its gnosis, is the Eternal One, God, the Sublime Reality, the Fount of Holiness.

324. "As for a description of God, you have asked for something impossible. For words cannot describe that which is unspeakable; It may only be known through inner communion.

"If I say that It is One, then this is recognised as truth by those who know It. But for those who have not yet known It, even the concept of oneness fails to reach Its sublime reality. For them, oneness indicates that It is one in opposition to the multiplicity of creation - yet it transcends such comparisons completely. It is the source of all qualities, all life, and all being. However, It is not like one quality or another, neither is It a mix of many qualities; It is beyond duality altogether. In truth, though people may seek to hear about It, nothing ultimately true can be said about It; for It can only be known through the direct communion of gnosis."

325. Sirr signalled again and then nodded. Ayah translated, "She said: This is what the great prophets and sages have told us; so please continue..."

The Wayfarer said, "The Divine Source is constantly outflowing like a blazing star, a bubbling spring and an eternal exhalation. So seek not words regarding It but know that It is The Unspeakable, Unspoken; for no word has ever touched Its sublime reality. So now sit in silent meditation, bathing in the radiance of Its Divine Outpouring."

326. Irfan then spoke again, saying, "I have become like an outpouring pitcher, filled with the light of communion, flowing with divine love to the multitude. Is there anything more left to attain?"

327. The Wayfarer said, "There are seven stages, the first of which is to witness the unspoken, unspeakable name of God. That is the first stage of communion but not communion in its entirety.

328. "The second stage is to witness the dance of universal gratitude. That is to say, the entire cosmos and all manifestations become a magnificent symphony of praise to The Sustainer of All Existence.

329. "The third is the great outpouring of Divine Love, and it is just as you have described; the heart begins to open to the light of communion, Divine Love overflows from it filling every cell - until it fills every hidden crevice of your awareness. It continues to increase in its intensity until you shall feel as if you have been pierced by the Unspeakable Name of the Sublime Majesty. Love begins overflowing from your very being with intense force and excruciatingly beautiful bliss. It flows from your limbs, from your eyes,

and every pore. That is a purification. It is a softening and a readying for the divine intimacy which is soon to come.

330. "The fourth stage is supreme gnosis, divine communion and inner-sight. It is a complete immersion in the Divine Essence, which takes place in the heart of the heart. In this state, the inner and the outer become as one. Meaning that just as in a dream, the person and the world in which they find themself are the same reality; as they are both constructs of mind and awareness. That is known as taking on the body of the cosmos. In this state, you shall see that the appearance of apparent multiplicity is an illusion; the dreamer and the dream are the same. O Irfan! Know that the inner and outer are the two eyes of the Universal Man, through which the reality of the cosmic self is seen.

331. "The fifth stage is peaceful surrender and the perfection of speech, which is no small matter, for it is through the word that the world and all experience is manifesting. So perfect the word within your heart, within your mind, and upon your lips. By doing so, you shall bring forth the beauteous reality and conquer all suffering.

332. "The sixth stage is the conformity of the limbs to the divine will."

Right at that moment, Irfan interjected, "But what are the limbs of the universal man?"

To which the Wayfarer continued, "Let me give you an example so that you might understand: When you were a babe you knew nothing of arms or hands. You saw them as external things that you could not control. You thought these strange things were incapable of changing the world around you. It was not until you realised that they were a part of you, that you began to learn to use them. So know that the limbs of the universal self are will and imagination. Yet you had taken them to be trivial and useless things. No! Indeed your duty to Good Thought is momentous! For what you call imagination, whether driven by fear or a good thought, is the hand which moulds your entire reality; by the power of the Divine Source.

333. "The seventh stage is the conformity of the mind and thoughts to the Divine outpouring and the absolute rejection of negative thoughts. The light of gnosis reaches up from the heart to the mind. Then, in an eternal moment, rapture takes hold, and you are returned to life; as if awaking from a deep sleep. At this point, you shall be like one who is given sight in a world of blindness; or you shall be like one given a lamp in a world of darkness. For you

shall be the vice-regent of God, and every thought shall dispense infinite goodness to all."

334. The female sage Nashwa (Rapture) opened her eyes, from deep meditation and asked, "What of heaven and hell, this life and the next?"

To which the Wayfarer replied, "First perfect this life, and you shall perfect that which is yet to come. 335. All of existence is like a fractal, repeating pattern; the small contains the immense, the vast contains the minute. That which manifests inwardly shall manifest outwardly. That which is within the seed shall become an endless forest.

"I ask you: What worth is paradise without gnosis, and what pain is hell to the enraptured soul? Indeed, the gardens of paradise are gnosis, pure unbounded awareness, and peaceful surrender to the Divine Source. Rivers of Good Thought run through them, as does rapture without intoxication, and sublime illuminated clarity. Once you have tasted the sweetness of this communion, nothing shall ever compare to it, and indeed, if you then became bereft of it, the heights of eternal paradise itself would become a wretched hell."

336. Nashwa then said, "O Wayfarer! You have answered me with that which I already knew. So now I will

ask that which I no longer know: Where does the Sublime Essence end, and where do I begin? For now, I tell you: Everywhere I look, all I see is The Face of the Sublime Oneness."

The Wayfarer said, "A question is a key to a locked door. Yet the door you stand on the precipice of is forever open and never closed. Therefore ask not, that which lips cannot explain, and minds cannot comprehend - instead, be."

CHAPTER 18

THE MIRACLE OF THE TREE

337. The Mystic Rayhan spoke saying, "In the teachings of the mystics of old, the wise prophets told of one who would arrive to overcome all that opposes good; one that would fill the world with prosperity, justice and Good Thought. 338. They taught that they would come with a flowering staff such as you yourself carry. They described it as a living staff and as a living tree. They explained that this tree that shall give eternal life to those who are baptised by its sap. Yet we look upon your staff with troubled hearts; for it is not a living tree, but rather a dead and dry stick.

339. The Wayfarer said, "Rayhan, are you still blinded by your belief in your doubts? Look with the eye of inner

sight and receive divine tuition. Beyond that which you have convinced yourself is an immutable reality."

340. The Wayfarer then took the flowering staff and forcefully pierced it into the earthen floor of the temple. 341. At once there was a rumbling in the earth, as roots began sprouting at a tremendous speed; twisting and turning through the soil. 342. The flower buds at the top of the staff became plump, looking like blazing stars, and released a pungent smell like sharp citrus and intoxicating musk. 343. Leaves and branches sprouted from the shaft of the staff which sprung to life as a beautiful, lush green tree. Its beauty was exceptional, such that everyone who looked upon it became instantly captivated by it. 344. The crowd murmured with a ripple of astounded voices as those who could see, reported the miraculous occurrence to those behind them, in an ever-expanding circle of voices. 345. Caressing the trunk and leaves of the tree, and looking at the Wayfarer with eyes overflowing with awe.

346. Rayhan, half whispering exclaimed, "O you! You *are* the promised one! I never knew I would be alive to meet you! I am not worthy of your presence!"

347. The Wayfarer said, "Dear one! Do not look at *me* with awe, but instead look solely toward the Unspeakable

Essence. I do not seek to become another barrier to supreme illumination - so cast me aside!

348. "Look at that which I have done, knowing that you shall do the same, and greater still. For with every turning spoke of the wheel, you shall rise to greater heights on the path to the ultimate summit. Remove every barrier until there is only the witness and the witnessed, then cast aside the idol of "I", for indeed that is the last idol."

Rayhan let her head fall back, with her arms flung open, sitting cross-legged on the floor; breathing deeply. Her face was beaming with a delighted smile, blissfully unaware of her surroundings.

CHAPTER 19

THE UNION OF THE MULTITUDE

349. By the time the miraculous event of the tree had come to pass, and the Wayfarer had finished speaking to Rahyan, every person in the kingdom had gathered in and around the temple. 350. The Wayfarer asked the King to find out if all the people had assembled.

Whilst the minds of the people entered deeply meditative states; the King sent out his entire court to find out if anyone was absent. 351. After many hours had passed the last of the attendants returned confirming that all one hundred and forty-four thousand people within the kingdom were in attendance: Men, women and children. 352. The Wayfarer slowly stood up within the deep stillness of the tranquillity, which had descended upon each and every heart. 353. Each movement held a peculiar and captivating sense of otherworldliness as the Wayfarer approached the tree, caressing the leaves and smelling the pungent scent.

354. Then grasping a sprig of flowers and cutting them from the tree with a small blade, the Wayfarer said, "This shall be our sacrificial goat, through which we shall slaughter our false personas and magnify within us the unspeakable name of God!"

355. Speaking to the King, the Wayfarer continued, "Bring us pure boiled water, so that we may wash ourselves of our iniquity."

The King spoke to his attendants in a soft voice, barely inaudible. After which they left, filled with great urgency.

356. After some time, the attendants returned with seven giant, steaming water pitchers.

The people moved back until there was room for them to be placed in front of the Wayfarer, who cast the flowers that had been cut from the tree into the pitchers, saying in a loud, melodic voice, "You who yearn to be baptised in the baptism of the divine presence; you shall imbibe this drink of unity.

"O people, open your hearts to the origin of all occurrences, with supreme optimism. Utter surrender shall uplift you like a chariot; to the unconditional intimacy of the secret of secrets. All actualities shall evaporate other than divine awareness. Ready yourselves for a remarkable journey; by seeking goodness in place of every reprehensible thought, word and deed that you have ever manifested. Enter the fount of effortless mercy, bathing yourselves in the endless waters of empathy and care. Take the path of total illumination, so that through thoughtfulness, you shall illuminate the world like a guiding torch. Harness inner harmony and heavenly insight, so that you may be a fountainhead of the greatest possible good. Elevate your enraptured essence to the throne of eternal ecstasy. Cultivate celestial communion through contemplation and meditative consciousness. Observe oneness with the Sublime Orchestrator, overwhelmed by Divine Love. Soar into the heights of sublimity, sanctified by the light arising within your soul. Meditate within the motionlessness of the silent mind; for in the midst of silence, you shall meet God. Obliterate obsessive clinging to individuation, opening to the reality of your original, authentic self. So that you may seek inner seclusion in the sacredness of intimacy with the unspeakable essence."

357. The attendants gathered one hundred and forty-four thousand cups each filled with water and a drop from each of the seven pitchers, then distributed the cups to each and every person.

Then the Wayfarer said, "Drink in the glory of the Divine Essence, and step through the doors of the heavenly abode."

358. As the one hundred and forty-four thousand lifted their cups, and drank from the waters therein, a great mystery descended upon them. Within that mystery, the one hundred and forty-four thousand cups became one cup. The one hundred and forty-four thousand beating hearts became one heart. The one hundred and forty-four thousand mouths became one mouth. The one hundred and forty-four thousand tongues became one tongue; undulating the divine word in rhythmic ecstasy. 359. One being, infinitely annihilating itself in the unfathomable mystery of itself. Light ascending into a more sublime light, again, and again without end - ascending as effortlessly as falling. Then, within the undulations of ecstatic realisation, the voice of knowing reverberated into awareness:

360. Be still, and witness the sublime name of God; unspeakable, unspoken. The one who proclaims it diverts

far from it; the one who knows it - is silenced by awe. Minds are not capable of encompassing it. Lips are not capable of uttering it. The heart is enraptured before it. Prostrate then, your entire being before the majesty of its Holy Mystery.

ABOUT THE AUTHOR

MY STORY

I am a Sufi Poet, Mystic and Qur'anic Gnostic from Southampton, England.

I have always been a seeker of The Divine, even since I was a young child. My life has been dedicated to the spiritual path, however, my spirituality really began to blossom when I encountered Sufi Islam. I took a Shaykh many years ago, which greatly benefited me. But it wasn't until Ramadan 2018 when I began to meditate solely on God, that I had a hugely profound spiritual experience of unity and direct inner communion, which has continued ever since.

My parents always encouraged me to express myself through the arts. My writing and poetry have taken many forms over the years, and sharing it with the world has been one of my greatest achievements. Since I began to share my poetry which is based on by direct spiritual experience and outflowing of Divine Love, I've never looked back. I have been constantly improving my poetic artistry and developing a soul touching style. My aim when writing, is for every world to be felt wholeheartedly by the reader, and to bring forth an inner connection to the soul, to love, and to The Divine Essence - God.

CONTACT DETAILS

To keep up to date with Lewis' poetry, book releases and other writings sign up to his VIP audience list at: www.lewisabdullahcattell.com

Email: info@lewisabdullahcattell.com

Wordpress: www.LewisAbdullahCattell.wordpress.com

Facebook: www.fcebook.com/lewisabdullahcattell

Instagram: www.instagram.com/lewis_cattell

Twitter: www.twitter.com/LewisACattell

Printed in Great Britain
by Amazon

60597061R00083